T0056718

EVERY DAY SHOULD BE

Valentine's ♥ Day

EVERY DAY SHOULD BE

Valentine's Day

Day

50 Inspiring Ideas and Heartwarming Stories
to Make Your Love Feel Special All the Time

Jennifer Basye Sander

Skyhorse Publishing

Copyright © 2020 by Jennifer Basye Sander

All rights reserved. No part of this book may be reproduced in
any manner without the express written consent of the publisher,
except in the case of brief excerpts in critical reviews or articles.
All inquiries should be addressed to Skyhorse Publishing,
307 West 36th Street, 11th Floor, New York, NY 10018.

Skyhorse Publishing books may be purchased in bulk at special
discounts for sales promotion, corporate gifts, fund-raising, or
educational purposes. Special editions can also be created to
specifications. For details, contact the Special Sales Department,
Skyhorse Publishing, 307 West 36th Street, 11th Floor,
New York, NY 10018 or info@skyhorsepublishing.com.

Skyhorse® and Skyhorse Publishing® are registered trademarks of
Skyhorse Publishing, Inc.®, a Delaware corporation.

Visit our website at www.skyhorsepublishing.com.

10 9 8 7 6 5 4 3 2 1

Library of Congress Cataloging-in-Publication Data is
available on file.

Cover design by Laura Klynstra
Cover image by gettyimages

Print ISBN: 978-1-5107-5231-3
Ebook ISBN: 978-1-5107-5232-0

Printed in China

Introduction

Welcome to the Every Day Is Special series! We're so glad you are here and ready to amp up the love, romance, and beauty in your life!

Valentine's Day has literally been around for centuries, ever since (as the legend goes) a monk named Valentine helped sweethearts send clandestine messages to each other. And then, as so often happens with a good idea, the business world got hold of it and boom—love and romance once a year becomes commercialized. From advertisements for jewelry to restaurant promotions promising an evening to remember, it can be easy to feel wiped out after the Valentine's Day commercial onslaught. Leaves a bit of a bad taste in the aftermath, doesn't it? So hey, take back your power! Celebrate every day instead!

Rest assured this is not a book about how to buy your way to a more romantic life. In compiling and collecting and creating these various ideas and suggestions, I have taken great care to consider any costs involved. What good is a book that suggests that you fly first class, enjoy fancy meals, and give diamonds as gifts? If you can afford any of these things, congratulations! However, if you are like most of us, those things would be a rare occurrence. Money stress is antiromance. Instead, we are here to help you *create* a more romantic life, and that requires *creativity*.

Where do fresh ideas for romance come from? From everything around you. Look at magazine pictures, or yes, Pinterest and Instagram. Don't look at these carefully staged images and think to yourself, *My life doesn't look like this and probably never will . . . I can't afford this, I can't go to that place, I can't visit that restaurant . . .* Instead, look creatively at what appeals to you and think to yourself, *How can I make my life look like this with what I already have?*

You and your partner will have different ideas about what is romantic, and that is okay. So much about being in a long-term relationship is about compromise, isn't it? And so we hope that both you and your partner get to indulge in the experiences and the moments that you each find romantic. Because if it always goes the way one of you wants it to, resentment might well bubble up.

The ideas and suggestions that we've collected here are not always about dewy-eyed romance, but often about having parallel experiences that bond you as a couple. Sprinkled throughout are also a handful of stories from people just like you about how even the most ordinary things can be viewed through a romantic lens. We've also included a handful of Romantic Splurges for those times when you have the cash on hand to do something wild. So read on, and see what new ideas appeal to you . . .

"We've got this gift of love, but love is like a precious plant. You can't just accept it and leave it in the cupboard or just think it's going to get on by itself. You've got to keep watering it. You've got to really look after it and nurture it."

-John Lennon

Save the Planet Together

Love and commitment require planning ahead, and what more romantic way to plan ahead than to do something for the benefit of future generations? Working together on projects is an important part of relationship harmony, so why not combine those two ideas and work together on saving the planet for future generations?

Join a "clean up the beach" day or volunteer to help out on a technology recycling day in your community. On the home front, make personal household goals together around things like composting food scraps, cutting back on energy use, or perhaps biking instead of using the car to get around.

What a great way to affirm the fact that you expect your relationship to go on and on and perhaps someday (or maybe you already have) bring in another generation of planet dwellers yourselves.

> Although every generation cares about the world, the newest among us are extremely focused on the topic. "Nothing dampens my mood faster than a partner who casually disrespects the planet we live on," says twenty-year-old Jonathan S. He went on to add, "and nothing earns my love and respect more than responsibility towards the only home we have."

Travel in Your Mind

♥

Much as we'd like to live fast-paced lives of romance and adventure, sometimes it is hard to find the time and energy to leave our own neighborhood. So how can you determine new ideas, new places, and new people to keep us interesting to ourselves and our partners? Well, you will just have to travel in your mind. Read a novel set in an exotic locale like retired attorney Pam Giarizzo has done.

Is there anything more romantic than traveling to an exotic paradise, quaint village, or world-class city? Having the opportunity to explore historic sites, meet interesting people, and sample new foods is an exhilarating experience but, unfortunately, time and money constraints mean you can't always just pick up and go to the exciting destinations you long to visit. Pam is taking an armchair journey around the globe by reading a book from every country in the world, and she shares her literary travels in her blog, "The Booktrekker." In addition to reading a book, she prepares a recipe and donates to a nonprofit organization doing work in each country. The hashtag #ReadCookGive describes Pam's approach to learning about places she may never actually visit in person, although after reading about some of these countries, she may have to add them to her bucket list! Look for "The Booktrekker" online.

"Will you come travel with me?
Shall we stick by each other as
long as we live?"

-Walt Whitman

Foot Massage Time

♥

Angela Montanez of New York shares what she thinks is wildly romantic—well, wildly romantic in front of the kids, anyway. "My brother-in-law very sweetly rubs my sister's back and feet every night after she has made dinner for the family. I think that is super romantic, and simple."

Simple, indeed. All you need is a willing partner and a bit of oil or lotion. A foot massage can be done—given or received (take turns, people)—while streaming your favorite show or talking about how your day went.

Here's an idea: can you try to combine the "four-minute look deep into your partner's eyes experiment" (page 44) with this? Giving or receiving a foot massage while looking steadily at your love . . . talk about amping up the intimacy! It might actually be too much to handle more than the one time you give it a try.

A Day of One's Own

♥

Everyone likes a celebration, so why not declare your own personal holiday? Not on your actual anniversary; choose another personal milestone. Maybe you will celebrate the first day of baseball season, or the day that your daffodils first bloom. Is this going to be a gift exchange event, or a romantic meal event, or perhaps a time to sneak away for a three-day weekend? It is your holiday, so you and your partner get to make the rules.

Your personal holiday can be a secret that you two share, or you could celebrate in a big way and go public. Throw a party with friends and let them in on your new holiday—chances are they'll want to create one, too!

Mix it Up

♥

Lovemaking is lovely, but it can sometimes grow a tad routine. The same old, same old . . . (In case this book falls into the hands of small children or your prudish aunt, we won't go into explicit detail here, but you get our drift.) So mix it up every so often!

There are abundant physical and emotional benefits to making love. Isn't it great to have science on our side (for once)? Not just doctors and scientists approve of having a healthy love life, but so does the business world. A recent study in *The Journal of Management* delivered an interesting result—that a happy, healthy sex life at home increases job satisfaction at work.

Another study, this one in *Psychological Science*, found that the "afterglow" of making love can last up to 48 hours, so that for the next two days, you feel the satisfying emotional effects of couple closeness.

"That love is all there is,
Is all we know of love."

-Emily Dickinson

Tub Time

♥

Bathtubs. Of course you know they are romantic, but who has the space or the money for a tub for two? Very few of us. So how do you share a romantic bath with what you already have? Well, what if you create the scene, using candles and flowers and big fluffy towels, and then only one of you is in the tub while the other reads aloud to you from a favorite book?

Use your imagination when it comes to the best books to read during tub time. Do you have a favorite book with a watery theme? Maybe a book about being stranded on a tropical island? The classics for those topics are *Treasure Island* by Robert Louis Stevenson and *Robinson Crusoe* by Daniel Defoe, which is frequently named as one of the 100 best books of all time. Just steer clear of something like Peter Benchley's *Jaws* . . .

Wild Romance

♥

Famed naturalist John Muir once described the great benefits of spending time outdoors like this: "Climb the mountains and get their good tidings. Nature's peace will flow into you as sunshine into trees." What a lovely image, something we need more of in these tumultuous times. So, where to find nature's peace? How about in one of our 8,565 state parks scattered across the United States!

State parks are a great backdrop for year-round (and pretty affordable) romance. With so many thousands to choose from, chances are there is one near you. Most of us have heard of some of the bigger state parks like Niagara Falls, but there are myriad smaller parks that don't get as much attention or visitors. Start looking around your own state to see what is available and begin your adventures. Buying a yearly admissions pass could bring you a full year of discovery.

"*Love is an irresistible desire to be irresistibly desired.*"

-Robert Frost

A Most Romantic Moment

I read a book. That was all I did, I read a book out loud. Okay, so it was a collection of erotic stories by Anaïs Nin, maybe that needs to be mentioned . . . Trying to think of how to make an ordinary afternoon with my love a bit more unusual, I rummaged around in my bookshelf until I found the perfect tool, the erotic story collection *Little Birds*. Nothing too crass or tacky, no actual sex described in cringe-worthy prose; instead, the author wrote lyrical and poetic pieces that let you fill in the blanks in your own mind.

I'm afraid it has been many years since then and I've forgotten the name of the story, but it had to do with a woman who comes home smelling like the spices from the spice market, and her husband takes a sudden romantic interest in her as a result. In order to heighten the atmosphere that afternoon, I'd also put a heavily spiced lamb roast in the oven to scent the air in the house as it cooked. The story, the smell of spices wafting through the air, it all combined to turn a perfectly regular day into one I still remember.

—Julia Berenson

Creative Cards

♥

You made cards for your mother when you were in pre-school, right? Touchingly homemade and amateurish efforts, sticky with glue and glitter. But her heart melted anyway, because you made it for her. So why not do the same for your partner? Time to return to your preschool ways and steer clear of premade cards.

At first you might fall back on quoting well-known poems, but if you make it a regular habit, you might well muster up the courage to write something more personal and heartfelt. Don't be held back by what you fear is your lack of talent. Crayons and glue make everyone smile. Or cut up a magazine and make a collage that sends a message. Don't be afraid of being laughed at—life itself is a risk, so go ahead and take one with your own creativity in order to show your love.

Get Lost

♥

Travel together somewhere that has no cell or Wi-Fi service. A place where you'd be wise to bring water, blankets, energy bars, and a solar-powered lantern . . . Just you two on a road, prepared for disaster but ready for anything. We spend so much time surrounded by comfort and ease, wouldn't you like to feel the teensiest bit tested? We aren't suggesting you two wander out into Death Valley with only a bottle of water between you, but rather that you give some thought to crafting an experience where you have to be a bit resourceful, and perhaps depend on each other's skills. Maybe for city dwellers that means trying your hand at backpacking on a mountain trail for a day or two; if you live in the country it might mean looking farther afield to parts of the state you haven't yet visited.

"We spent a week together at a remote cabin in the high desert," Beanie Carr told us, "and I was totally surprised to see that my partner knew how to get a generator running. And he was surprised that I knew how to fish—I'd learned from my father. We were about twenty miles from a cell signal, which felt strange but we got used to it. It just might become an annual ritual for us!"

A great resource for researching camping and hiking ideas is trails.com. You can choose the type of activity that interests you, type in your zip code, and it will generate info on all of the choices near you.

Take a Local Tour

♥

Travel is romantic, we all know that. But travel can also be expensive, and really only an occasional treat to be budgeted for and carefully planned. So what can we do while waiting for the big trips to happen? Why not be a tourist in your own town?

Standard romantic marketing images use gaudy photos of Paris, Hawaii, or the Caribbean. And romance novels take place more often in the English countryside than in an ordinary town like most of us live in. Wait, though . . . your own town, your own state, is full of romantic possibilities and new ways to explore.

Envy another neighborhood in your town? Become a resident there for a night anyway, by finding a place on Airbnb in that area, and see what it is like to live there. Airbnb has done a deep dive into offering "Experiences" in addition to just places to stay. Check and see what kinds of local experiences are available on their site: food tours, history tours, or maybe a cooking class. Staying in another part of town or taking a tour with another local resident will give you the chance to see your own town through fresh eyes.

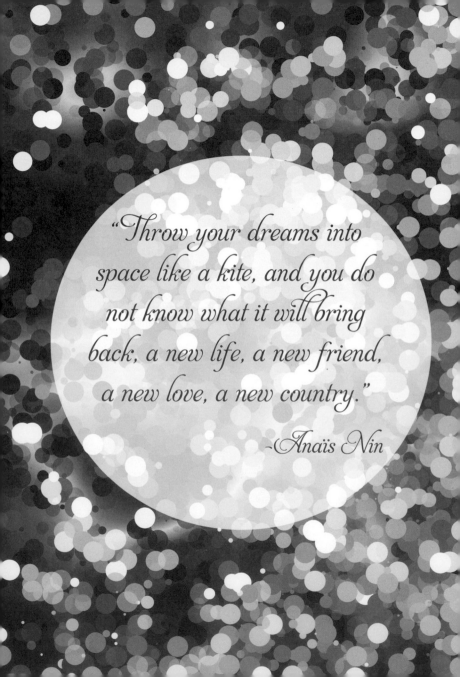

"Throw your dreams into space like a kite, and you do not know what it will bring back, a new life, a new friend, a new love, a new country."

-Anaïs Nin

Experiment Together

♥

No, we don't mean you should experiment with hallucinogenics, but maybe you could dip your collective toes into veganism for a week. Listen to a new style of music? Skinny dip in a secluded pool? Try an international cuisine you've never before tasted? Daily life can get dull and grow routine; it is bound to happen. Unless you actively try to shake things up a bit by trying to do things differently every so often.

Go ahead, try something new tonight. Experiment in some small way and then build up to something on a larger scale. Remember that all great discoveries came as a result of experimentation!

A Most Romantic Moment

The most romantic thing my partner Bill ever did was see me. From the beginning, he took note of even the smallest details of my habits and then made it his job to please me. He not only learned my coffee order (grande hazelnut mocha, no whip) and had it waiting for me when I got out of the gym, he mastered making it in the morning and brought it to me in bed while I scrolled through my phone. I could taste the love in it.

Now, he could have pointed out how many calories and grams of sugar were in my beverage of choice and mounted a campaign to persuade me to adopt a healthier option. Or he could have extolled the benefits of drinking the robust roast he preferred, black. But he didn't. He respected my choice. And I love him for that.

His "observe-and-fulfill" approach to our relationship went way beyond coffee, however. He quickly learned my favorite music, restaurants, and movie types and was quick to suggest them whenever appropriate. Pretty early in our dating history, when were just entering the stage where we left things at each other's house, he earned his superhuman stripes for being thoughtful. I had left a box of tampons in the supply closet as a "just-in-case" measure. He noticed that the box was almost empty and went to the store to purchase the exact brand and type I used. The thought of his six-foot-tall silhouette standing in that grocery store aisle staring at shelves of pink squares, discerning between the "supers" and "sports" and "ultras" to get just the right box, still melts my heart. This is a man who blushes at the drop of a compliment. But he did this for me. And he didn't announce it. He quietly slipped it in the closet so it would be there when I needed it.

Bill sees all of me and still loves me. It doesn't get much more romantic than that.

—JT Long

Roses Are Forever

♥

What could be more romantic than a lush garden filled with roses? The rose has long symbolized love and romance, and designing and then planting a rose garden together is a delightful and long-lasting way to create a symbol of your love. Angela Montanez was touched by one man's romantic technique: "He came and planted roses around my property. He knew I loved the various colors and said that instead of buying me roses that will die, he'd plant them and then I could enjoy them as they bloom in the warmer months and bring them inside to enjoy. He planted white, pink, and red roses, and yes, I enjoy them every year when they bloom. When it comes to colors, choose pinks, reds, and also scents that stimulate your brain and direct it toward love."

Roses come in an overwhelming assortment of colors, sizes, and shapes. And they have wonderful names: "Sugar Baby," "Buff Beauty," "Maiden's Blush," to list just a few examples. You might be able to plan and then plant a garden in which the roses secretly tell your own personal love story . . . maybe commemorate an afternoon on the beach with "Sunset Memory," or a honeymoon in Paris with "La Reine." The more thought you put into your plant choices, the more personal your rose garden can be.

True Mastery

♥

Think that life used to be more adventurous and exciting back in the day? Back in *which* day, exactly? Back when there were undiscovered jungles to explore, new mountains to conquer, back in the day of famous explorers like Ernest Shackleton or writers like Ernest Hemingway and Zane Grey, who drank and fished all over the world? Our lives seem so tame and well-ordered by comparison. We need to undergo some adventurous challenges!

Bestselling writer Geoffrey Gray decided to try to revive some of that adventurous spirit and founded True Mastery, a website that issues all manner of challenges to its followers. He describes it as "The path to a full and adventurous life." You can sign up to participate at truemastery.me.

Recent challenges were Embrace the Dawn, which challenged folks to get up early and photograph the sunrise. You can do that, right? A simple task that you two can plan together, decide which scene you are going to photograph, set the alarm, and—action. Doesn't sound like much of a challenge for folks who have to get up early anyway, or the parents of small children. Other challenges include the Perfect Martini Challenge. You can make one of those easily, we are certain. Start with those simple sorts of challenges, and then you might move on to joining a team trying to find hidden treasure or meeting up with other members to parachute out of an airplane.

A Most Romantic Moment

On his cross-country business trips, my husband, Tom, slowly gathered a clan of stuffed animals. By the time they reached our home in Northern California, each was introduced to me with a full name and complete backstory. They had furniture, clothing, and at one time lived in individually staged environments in a "condominium" he built on the living room wall.

The patriarch of the plush family was Rudy Olaf, Alpine skier. He was about the size of a cantaloupe, pudgy and dog-like with long ears, and a squeaker in his tummy. He was made of pastel-colored rip-stop fabric used for sportswear. Tom said he was built for speed and had competed in the Winter Olympics in Albertville, France.

One night in December, Tom, Rudy, and I went to San Francisco to see the holiday lights. We stayed in the penthouse of an old downtown hotel. At 2:00 a.m., Tom woke me, saying in a calm voice, "Ingrid, there's a fire in the hotel. Put on your clothes and tennis shoes; get Rudy and your flashlight."

The alarm was loud in the hallway when we entered the stairwell on the 23rd floor. We cautiously wound our way down and watched the floor numbers get smaller. At the third floor, the stairwell opened onto a wide hallway with smoke so thick it was hard to see and breathe. In the confusion we separated, but Tom found me in seconds by a window, and we made our way to the last set of exit stairs.

The door at the end of those stairs opened into an underground delivery tunnel filled with frightened hotel guests in varying states of dress. Above the clatter of languages, we heard sirens and saw revolving flashes of red through cracks in the door.

When the firemen broke the lock and flung open the doors, we all rushed out into the night chill and a deserted street illuminated only by neon signs and the dim yellow glow of streetlights. The cops told us that a transient had snuck into the hotel elevator and rode it up and down, stopping to set fires in garbage cans on several floors.

'It's okay. Our family is safe,' Tom said as he hugged me, and from under my shirt Rudy squeaked in reply.

—Ingrid Lundquist

Devices Be Gone!

♥

This is hardly new advice, but we find it hard to take this advice ourselves. Put the devices away at night. This is hard, but all of those studies about how our various tech devices interrupt healthy sleep patterns and add a layer of constant stress are true. Decide together on a policy and give it a tryout period. What will you do instead of reading your iPads next to each other in bed? Hey, you could talk about how the day went. You could share a laugh. You could turn off the light and . . . oh, you know. Because remember, if you are in bed holding a device, you aren't holding each other.

"Knowing how to be solitary is central to the art of loving. When we can be alone, we can be with others without using them as a means of escape."

-bell hooks

Keep Bubbly at the Ready

Champagne is the universal drink of romance, no doubt due to the decades of marketing efforts of the major champagne producers. And of course an occasional splurge on a pricey bottle of Bollinger, Veuve Cliquot, or Moët & Chandon is a treat. But why deprive yourself of a bubbly drink in between splurges? Make it a point to always have a bottle of prosecco and rosé in the fridge for a relaxing end-of-the-day or end-of-the-week moment to share with your partner. Whereas a good bottle of champagne hovers in the fifty-dollar range, a fine bottle of prosecco is affordable on a more regular basis.

Lily Bollinger, who ran the family champagne company after her husband died in WWII, is quoted as saying, "I drink champagne when I'm happy and when I'm sad. Sometimes I drink it when I'm alone. When I have company I consider it obligatory. I trifle with it if I'm not hungry and drink it when I am. Otherwise I never touch it—unless I am thirsty."

Southern California-based sommelier Roxanne Langer recommends replacing bubbly for wine with dinner on occasion: "Champagne pairs well with anything briny, which is why oysters and champagne are such a classic combo. Also works well with seafood in a cream sauce, the acidity of the champagne cuts through the fat in the butter."

Champagne Is
for the Ladies

Champagne is literally girl power in a glass. Several of the major French champagne houses have been run by powerful women who shaped their history. Veuve Cliquot was run by the widow of the founder, and Madame Cliquot is not only credited with creating the first known blended rosé champagne, but also in creating the marketing mystique that turned champagne into the preferred drink in upper crust society. And if that weren't enough, she is also known for her bravery—once smuggling 10,000 bottles across several countries in order to beat competitors into an emerging market in Russia. Bollinger, Pommery, Henriot, and Laurent-Perrier were also all run by women at some point in their history. So let's drink a toast in their honor!

Manners Matter

♥

Your mother, and no doubt your mother's mother, gave you this advice over and over: Manners *do* matter. Manners also are a factor in how we feel about the people we spend time with, most particularly our partners. Good manners are sexy. So go on and use your best manners in public and in private and encourage your partner to do their part, too.

One of the most polite ways to behave in conversation is to be attentive to whoever is speaking. Attentiveness in the form of turning toward the speaker and looking at them while they speak. And when it is your turn to talk, looking toward them when you are speaking. Very simple advice, but one that brings big results when practiced. You and your partner will both benefit.

A Most Romantic Moment

Laughter is always the best aphrodisiac, and my husband, Haskell, and I laughed a lot. Speeding down the coast in his beloved Acura NSX, listening to music and singing along to Bon Jovi's "Blaze of Glory," or a Neil Young song, or one of our favorites, Prince's version of Joni Mitchell's "A Case of You."

But best of all was the song "Precious Friend," by the folk singer/songwriter Pete Seeger. Haskell loved this and we sang it together, and once we sang it with Pete Seeger himself. When it came time to plan a memorial for my Haskell, I played it at his memorial so the audience of friends and family could sing along.

—Rita Taggert

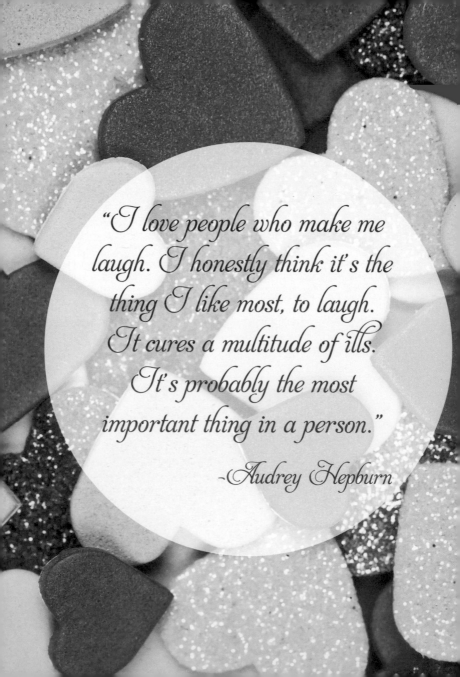

"I love people who make me laugh. I honestly think it's the thing I like most, to laugh. It cures a multitude of ills. It's probably the most important thing in a person."

-Audrey Hepburn

Back to School

♥

Change is what keeps life interesting. Change is what keeps romance fresh and alive. So go back to school together for a change. Learn a new skill, or study a new topic. Not everyone wants to take an evening class in film appreciation, but what about an afternoon-long class on a new cooking technique? And this is your chance to show an interest in things that your partner is interested in. Conversely, it is also your partner's chance to show an interest in what YOU like.

> The national outdoor sports and recreation chain REI offers outdoorsy skill classes at their stores, like Introduction to Outdoor Photography, and Stand Up Paddleboarding. There are even classes for city folk like Urban Emergency Preparedness. Check out the classes near you at rei.com.

A Most Romantic Moment

Detroit, 1986 . . . Gloves of white lace, hand-stitched, vintage. I kept staring at them in the glass case (craning my neck around all the gaudy jewelry and baubles), knowing that I was sure-as-hell going to have to buy those gloves, no matter how much they cost! The wedding was just weeks away, and Sandra said nothing about wanting or needing a five-dollar pair of antique gloves to complete her wedding day ensemble. She had the dress—paid $100 for it at the Polish wedding shop on Michigan Ave. Sandra came out of the fitting room, pressing down the bodice, her hips feeling its fullness, the fabric, in all its curlicue, posh-paisley lace, and I gasped. Her college friend Lisa caught her breath, both hands covering her mouth. She and I simultaneously uttered, "Oh!" It was a moment of shared awe. Sandra's panicked voice questioned, "What?" And all I could manage was "You're lovely," then caught myself. Days later, the wide, double doors of Saints Peter and Paul church open, and Sandra was there, waiting. Smiling, she extended her hand, and mine reached out to meet it. I felt the softness and the delicate stitching of her gloved hand.

—Ruben Mauricio

Romance Yourself First

♥

Inspirational speaker Angela Montanez describes herself as "an inner alchemist," one who creates a self-loving alchemical ritual for the mind, body, and soul that aligns you to receive love in all forms on a daily basis. "I like to romance myself first," she says, "and in the time of rising empowerment of the divine feminine, self-love can help you accept and appreciate receiving love from another." Here are some ideas from Angela's self-love list:

- Diffuse rose oil (or your favorite scent) every night and throughout the day.
- Paint a wall (or two) your favorite romantic color—like a soft pale pink.
- Purchase light, soft, flowery, earthy, or sultry scents to wear any time.
- Sprinkle your living space with lots of rose quartz crystals, carnelian, and any stone that whispers love.
- Hang wilting roses or flowers to dry upside down in bunches around your home or in small vases.

Angela shares the romantic advice that her father once gave her: "I like my dad's perspective on love. My dad always said, 'life with your significant other should be an adventure,' so find the adventure in the everyday and the romance will blossom from it."

Keep Talking

A few years back, the popular *New York Times* column "Modern Love" ran an essay by Mandy Len Catron, "To Fall in Love with Anyone, Do This." Big promise, eh? The essay contained the 36 questions that, if you and a partner worked through the questions together, would result in closeness and intimacy. This was all based on the work of psychologist Arthur Aron, who studied intimacy and discovered that mutual vulnerability creates closeness. To quote from the study itself, even strangers can create a sense of immediate closeness by using ". . . sustained, escalating, reciprocal, personal self-disclosure."

The questions themselves ranged from describing what you think is a perfect day, to sharing your most treasured memory, to then sharing your most terrible memory. You can find them online by searching for 36 Questions that Lead to Love.

The bottom line is, keep talking to your partner. Keep revealing yourself. Keep asking questions that allow them to reveal themselves. Keep working on that mutual vulnerability thing. Because even if you are already in love, there is always a chance to deepen the connection.

Don't think that every conversation with your partner needs to deepen your connection, though; even a simple "How was your day?" gives the other person a chance to share and then, hopefully, ask you about your day in return.

"You yourself, as much as anybody in the universe, deserve your love and attention."

-Mahatma Gandhi

Your Turn to Choose

♥

Do something your partner loves, that you are . . .perhaps less than enthusiastic about. And mix it up so that you get to do what you like but they might not be wild about. So maybe one weekend you can attend a Broadway musical one night and a monster truck pull the next. Or go wine tasting on a Saturday afternoon and then spend Sunday afternoon at a brewpub. Because life is about contrasts, right? And love is about compromise.

Fill a jar with small scraps of paper on which you've written ideas on how to spend a day, or an evening, or maybe just an hour. Each of you should write out at least twenty ideas, making sure that it is an equal number that you each contribute so that the chances are fifty-fifty when an idea is drawn out. Mix them up and start pulling out ideas!

This might be something as simple as "have a movie marathon," or "Go to a new brewery." Agree to a few rules before you start generating ideas, like "Keep it legal, keep it cheap, keep it safe," and then keep your life interesting!

Sleep Station

♥

Perhaps you've heard about the advice from the bestselling author Admiral William H. McRaven (Ret.) in his book *Make Your Bed: Little Things That Can Change Your Life . . . and Maybe the World*. Because this simple and mundane daily task gives you a sense of accomplishment at the very start of the day. And that sense of achievement can help move you forward to accomplish more and more throughout the rest of the day. Because you set the tone right from the beginning. Now, what if we take that motto one step further and say, "Make your bed with good sheets" in order to set the tone for your evening hours?

Sliding between a new set of sheets is a sensuous thrill. Far cheaper than a stay in a swanky hotel, you can redo your bed linens and enjoy that sensuous feeling every single night at home.

High thread-count sheets run the gamut in terms of pricing—if you want to enjoy the very top end product but blanche at the price, what about splurging on just a pair of pillow cases in a lux brand?

A Most Romantic Moment

One of the most difficult things about traveling is leaving our pets behind. Because we never had children, they are our "kids," and we long for that type of connection when trips take us to faraway places. Pet sitting makes an otherwise ordinary outing into a truly extraordinary and romantic adventure.

Since we retired and have been living on a fairly rigid budget, volunteer pet sitting with trustedhousesitters.com has become our new way of travel. It not only allows us to be with furry friends on the road, but it also provides a sense of relief when we use the service for our pets back home. We love to cuddle with cats and trek on trails with dogs. We've even cozied up to pigs and chickens, donkeys, and ducks, in amazing settings like French châteaux. The meals we've shared, the wines we've enjoyed, the places we've stayed, all thanks to pet sitting. Life doesn't get much more romantic than that.

—Karen Shuppert

Jammie Time

♥

In the same way that a new set of sheets can feel like a massive indulgence, a new pair of pajamas can also be a small treat with a big payoff. Do you find yourself slipping into bed night after night in the same well-worn thing? Our brains need stimulation, remember that. So even if all you do is buy a new colored top to wear with the same bottoms, you are changing up the scenery.

So head out now, or go online, and see how you can change your nighttime scenery. Why not change what you are looking at too, and get a new nighttime outfit for your bed partner? Even if you sleep sans clothing, a change of scenery might be in order there, too. Throw on a night-shirt, slip on some socks, anything to change up your routine a bit.

A Most Romantic Moment

Being an eternally hopeful romantic, my lifelong passion for jewelry has more to do with the people and the story behind whatever piece I'm creating, appraising, buying, or selling, than it does with the monetary value of the piece. What I never realized I would grow to appreciate even more than the people celebrating an engagement or marriage is the gift that I am able to give to members of my community when their family member passes. The saddest of times—loss of a parent, sibling, child, or best friend—is when the very same people for whom I've made talismans as tokens of their loyalty and love come to me first, to my great surprise. They give me the honor of helping them sort through what remains, in terms of jewelry.

One day, a man who moved to California from Ireland fifty years ago came to my store with two grocery bags of mostly costume jewelry. He told me how both his wife and her sister emigrated with him. How, for the past twenty-five years, they made friends, led many community enrichments, raised children, helped with the grandchildren. But now, both his wife and her sister were close to death.

I sorted the contents of the bags for him. I took out some notebook paper, sorted and cleaned each piece, numbered them, made lists, and listened intently, writing down his stories as I told him the provenance of each piece. His memories flooded back as I identified the make of each piece of jewelry he had given his wife or she bought herself, and why, over all those years.

His daughter came to my store soon after to thank me for helping her father sort out his memories, using the tokens of his great love for his bride and his ancestors and living family, in the form of jewelry, as catalysts to get him to talk about memories too painful or difficult for him to tell them as the wife and her sister were suffering. They thanked me for writing down the stories about the talismans of love that transcended the death of the mother that very same morning. They told me that their dad read them and their mother the stories and the descriptions I wrote as she was breathing her last breaths. That "stuff" wasn't just jewelry. It was their family's talismans. Evoking memories of the long and passionate love between a man and his wife, their emigration from war-torn Ireland to the US, and what ended up being five generations of stories.

I am always grateful that I have the most precious gift available to give: my time. Time, our only nonrenewable commodity, and forty-plus years of studying all aspects of jewelry and gems enabled me to memorialize, preserve, and pass forward what that man had told me.

—Andrea Riso

The Look of Love

♥

In the 36 questions challenge mentioned on page 36, the final step is not actually a question. Instead, it is a challenge. You are challenged to look silently into each other's eyes for a sustained period of time—for four minutes without looking away. Mandy Len Catron, author of the essay that popularized the 36 questions, describes her experience this way: "I've skied steep slopes and hung from a rock face by a short length of rope, but staring into someone's eyes for four silent minutes was one of the most thrilling and terrifying experiences of my life."

Sound like a relationship-building exercise you'd like to try? Discuss it with your partner, get their agreement to give it a try, pick a quiet spot where you aren't likely to be disturbed, and let the staring begin!

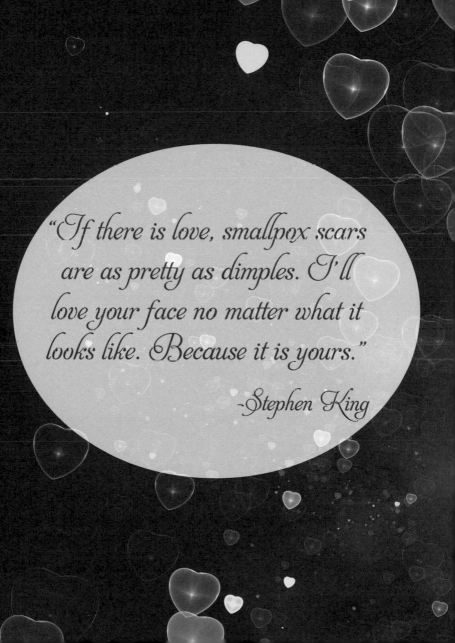

"If there is love, smallpox scars are as pretty as dimples. I'll love your face no matter what it looks like. Because it is yours."

-Stephen King

Water World

♥

What is it about a body of water that seems to create romance in a way few other natural sights do? At the ocean, the waves roll in and out like a heartbeat; on a river, the current flows endlessly out to faraway destinations. Ah yes, whether you are snuggling together in the back of a Venetian gondola, or under an umbrella at a secluded beach, the idea of being on, or near, the water is always romantic. Unless you or your partner are afraid of the water, in which case you can skip this idea. If you have access to unlimited funds, of course, you can charter a boat or book a cruise through the Mediterranean. If you are like the rest of us, though, your watery jaunt might be as simple as taking a commuter ferry ride together or even a tourist boat in your own town. After all, even native Parisians on occasion jump onto the Bateaux Mouches and cruise down the Seine like tourists.

Remy Kenny founded her company, The Honey Fitz Yacht Club, in order to help create a watery vibe no matter where you happen to live. "The thing about the water," she told us, "is it appeals to all your senses. It grabs your attention right away, as soon as you step foot on the sand, board a boat, smell the salty air, or feel the sea breeze on your skin. It's hard to be distracted when you are by the water, allowing you to concentrate exactly on where you are and who you're with. At sunrise, the whole day lays out in front of you. Quiet, optimistic, reassuring. At sunset, there's nothing standing in between you, your loved one, and a perfectly poured cocktail. It doesn't get more romantic than that.

"At home I surround myself with art and objects that remind me of the enchantment of being by the water. I have more seashells than I can count and collect coral every chance I get. I don't think it matters if you live by the coast or in the middle of the country. If you find a conch shell that reminds you of your honeymoon or just a lazy day in the sand, it deserves a spot on your shelf."

Get a Smaller Bed

♥

Lounging around on a huge king-sized bed might seem like ever couple's ultimate goal, but here is romance advice straight from a woman who has been married for nearly sixty years: Judith Viorst, the author of *Alexander and the Terrible, Horrible, No Good, Very Bad Day* and many other bestselling books, was asked by a *New York Times* reporter for the secret to a long and happy marriage. "It's a double bed! You can't get away from each other," she said. "You can't sulkily move to your end and not have your tushies touching."

There is a great deal of wisdom in that, isn't there? In any kind of small space—a car, a room, or a bed—you need to work things out and come to an agreement faster than if there were room to spread out and get away from each other.

Practice Wabi-Sabi
and Kintsugi

♥

Looking around your life every day and only noticing what is wrong, what is broken, is antiromance. Being able to look at what surrounds us with an eye toward appreciating flawed beauty takes us many steps closer to living a romantic life. Wabi-sabi is a Japanese tradition that emphasizes the acceptance of the transience and imperfection of daily life. Nothing lasts, nothing is finished, nothing is perfect. So instead of getting frustrated that your Wi-Fi signal isn't strong this morning or that you are out of coffee yet again, hey, that's wabi-sabi. Nothing is perfect. Think of it as the philosophical embodiment of the way your heart melts when a small child hands you a scribbled drawing. Far from perfect, messy, deeply flawed, but we see the beauty right away. Daily life is like that child's drawing, slightly offbeat and far from perfect but beautiful nevertheless.

Kintsugi is an ancient method of Japanese repair in which the repair is made both visible and beautiful. A cracked ceramic tea cup is fixed with an obvious stream of gold metal holding it together, recognizing the history of the item and incorporating a visible repair rather than trying to make it perfect again. If we try to think of ourselves and our relationships as the cracked vessel, can we fix what is broken in a beautiful and obvious way rather than trying to quietly fix things and hope that they will be perfect again?

A Most Romantic Moment

How do you know when someone loves you? It's the everyday things. The small gifts of time spent together, emptying the dishwasher when it's not your turn, holding a hand in companionable silence. It is also the small things given when it's not a holiday or your birthday: flowers because they can't remember the last time they gave you flowers, a note on a pillow or in a suitcase when you are parted from each other.

For years, my husband and I have been involved in Renaissance Faires and Dickens Faires, but lately I've become enamored of a stylish Australian mystery series set just after World War I. Bone pins are a California Renaissance Faire tradition. They are collected, given as gifts, hidden away inside costumes if the message if not "period appropriate." Yet here in my suitcase were three bone pins he had made for me for another reason entirely, all because of a certain Lady Detective.

It is bone pins given to you because you watch *Miss Fisher's Murder Mysteries* and you have found a community of people who love it as much as you. And you may have shown your spouse and child this show a time or two. Or six. Or as many times as it took for your spouse to commit lines somewhat to memory and have bone pins commissioned for you. It is letting you go to Australia alone to get even deeper into the Miss Fisher world and the fan community. You didn't need to ask permission, but there are so many details to consider when one half of a partnership leaves on an adventure, half-way around the world, without the other half.

In the series, when Miss Fisher leaves her love and boards a rickety plane, she was wearing a pin in the shape of a swallow that her love interest had given her, as a promise that she would return. I too was wearing a pin as I boarded a significantly less rickety jumbo jet. My husband had it made for me.

—Jennifer Aldrich

Be Brave and Write a Poem

Have you ever tried your hand at writing a poem or two? Free verse, no need to worry about rhyme or meter.

We asked poet Karen Durham for a quick lesson: "You want to bare your soul," she says, "You must be either very brave, or in love. Let me walk you through one of the ways I build a poem. This one is to my longtime love.

"Touch your pen to paper. Start with a 'thing.' My thing here is my love for my husband. Your thing can be any feeling—any emotion, moment, or an epiphany, if you will. Describe your thing without saying the thing. For instance, let's choose a dragonfly—the way a dragonfly is only visible for one impossible instant. What is your physical reaction? Then blink and it's gone. Your mind's camera snaps a grainy picture. Write what you see. This is the poem's foundation—it will become your joy and despair as you work it in ever smaller spirals until at last your thing is at its essence. You have said nothing. You have not said your thing, yet have said everything. Now put your poem in a drawer, and leave it for a week, or even a year. When it emerges, the real poetry begins. You'll find your poem is a stranger to you, most of it meaningless, or trite, and you'll ask yourself, 'Who wrote this?' But be kind, touch your pen to it again, underline every word and phrase that pleases you, speaks to you. Write only these, and here find your poem."

MY LOVE

♥

for you when we met hovers,
an unseen damselfly, its
reflection paused on still water.

Impossible, this
                    instant.

Unsure what I see, I
gasp   blink   it's gone.

All that remains is
silverhot on my skin, an
exposure stain.

I spiral into its least
essence, leave nothing,
leave everything.

I trap my damselfly in a jar
until a lifetime passes, until
it emerges   a stranger.

As iridescent as ever, it
bears no resemblance to
the thing I bottled.

—Karen Durham

Haiku is perhaps the least intimidating form of poetry. You remember it from grade school, don't you? It's a Japanese literary form in which the first line contains five syllables, the second line contains seven syllables, and then the final line reverts to five again. Not 5-7-5 words, mind you, but syllables. Once you start counting it out, you will see how very easy it is to write a haiku for your partner. We promise.

Money Matters

♥

Fighting about money is antiromance. Hiding info from each other about just how much you are in debt is antiromance. In fact, one of the most loving things you can do is level with your partner about your financial situation. And vice versa: you need to have a clear eye of what the financial boundaries are for both of you in order to not create stress.

A study conducted by Experian looked at recently divorced adults and learned that 20 percent of them said that money stress played a big role in their divorces. Almost half said their credit score worsened during marriage.

So have these tough, but necessary, conversations about finances. Money talk doesn't sound romantic, but bravely undertaking regular money talk might in fact be the most romantic thing you can do for your relationship.

"One of the most loving and heartfelt things my partner ever did was admit that his generosity toward me—little gifts and trips and splurges on a weekly basis—was becoming a financial problem. He was relieved to be able to tell me about it. He was worried that if he just stopped that pattern I would think he'd lost interest in me. Far from it: when he told me the truth I felt more loved than ever. A flower he plucked from our garden is more romantic than a night out at the newest cocktail lounge," an anonymous friend told us.

Go ahead and have a cup of coffee from your favorite coffee shop. Don't fall for the guilt-inducing ads about how you should be investing that money instead. You need small pleasures in your daily life. Find another place to trim your budget.

"We are reminded that, in the fleeting time we have on this Earth, what matters is not wealth, or status, or power, or fame, but rather how well we have loved and what small part we have played in making the lives of others better."

-Barack Obama

A Most Romantic Moment

When it seems things can get no worse, I try to imagine someone suffering even more.

But I had never felt the marrow-deep fatigue like the weekend my boyfriend and I moved from Washington, DC, to his hometown of Bowling Green, Kentucky. I was overjoyed, but as I slumped over those *last two* boxes (trash bags, at this point), sciatica wailing, I felt I could not go on. Breaking up with him would take less energy.

Moving was hard on Wes, too. My college friend from some twenty-five years before, he was now a divorced attorney and father of three still struggling to walk after breaking his back in a car accident. The first time we reconnected on the phone, Wes admitted he had a permanent limp, no longer the strapping college football lineman I once knew. Hey, I was a never-married writer, I joked—whose handicap was worse?

A year later, this spinster and her gimpy guy merely needed to pack and haul forty-seven years of life across three states in the one free weekend Wes had before the start of a historic murder trial in which he was cocounsel.

The drive was full of laughter and music and greasy spoon coffee. I didn't sleep because I wanted to help him navigate. And I wanted to remember every moment. A photo of us beneath a giant Davy Crockett statue at some Tennessee truck stop shows someone I barely recognize. Me, so tired. And so happy.

When we finally arrived that arctic January morning, we had to immediately unpack and return the U-Haul to avoid a steep late fee. I made some coffee, sobbed in the bathroom, then rolled up my sleeves.

But Wes waved me off and steered me to the bed. "You just rest. I've got this," he said. He made me some tea, lit a candle, and closed the door.

When I woke six hours later, the truck was gone. We've had many lovely dinners since then, but none better than the ramen noodles I sat and ate, looking at my furniture now in his—our—house and knowing my new life with this perfect (for me) man had finally begun.

—Laura Boswell

Beauty Squared

♥

All we can really control in life is our own moods, how we feel at any given moment, or how we react to those feelings. And in those moments when you are feeling low, like your life is humdrum and drab and nothing will ever change . . . why not pause and look for the beauty around you?

Cut a small square-shaped hole into a piece of paper and look through it as though through a camera lens. Crop the world in such a way that you can see and focus on the beauty. You will see your life and your surroundings in a sharper way.

You can zoom in with the camera in your phone in order to crop a scene and create a beautiful image anytime you want. Just don't forget that you can do that at any moment you need to in life: just zoom your mental focus in on a small detail to enjoy when everything else seems out of control.

Think of it as a bit of personal Instagramming—in the same way you'd frame some small bit of beauty to share with (or impress) your friends, you are using the filters in your mind's eye to see the world in a different way.

Move Outdoors

♥

Being outdoors is good for us: we all know that, right? In Japan, they have taken that casual belief to a higher plane and since the 1980s have touted "forest bathing" as a cornerstone of preventive health care and healing. The sounds of nature, the smell of trees and the forest floor, the way the sun dapples the leaves . . . we relax and breathe a bit more deeply, don't we? You are forest bathing anytime you are outdoors in a natural setting.

Forest bathing plus eating outdoors: sounds like we need a new term for that, don't we? Dining alfresco, or maybe plain old "picnicking," whatever you call it, eating outside is always a treat. Add in a little candlelight to amp up the atmosphere for you and your partner, and your alfresco picnic is complete. Bon appétit!

Create a Very Small Book Club

♥

You might already belong to a book club in your neighborhood or church, but why not have your own private book club with your partner? Choose a book that you will both enjoy reading, or perhaps take turns choosing the book that one of you enjoys and the other might have to stretch a little to fully absorb. Because that is what couple-dom is all about, learning each other's tastes and interests and then possibly expanding your own to include theirs.

Alternatively, if you do belong to a book club now, perhaps the other members would be open to having at least one meeting a year when you all brought your spouses to read and discuss the book?

Longtime book club member Donna Erkel had this to say about a meeting where the members brought their husbands to meet A.J. Baime, author of the book *The Accidental President: Harry Truman and the Four Months that Changed the World*: "I have participated in my book group for more than twenty years. The other women know me intimately but so little about my husband. As a change in our routine we invited our partners to join us when we hosted the author of a history book. Toward the end of the meeting Al spoke up to express a contrarian position. In that moment, I loved and admired him so much for his unassuming sense of intelligence, knowledge of the subject, his reasoned sense of social justice, and the courage to express it."

"Pull up a chair.
Take a taste.
Come join us.
Life is so endlessly
delicious."

-Ruth Reichl

Very Vintage

♥

Vintage men's accessories are very cool and romantic gifts. Matt Hranek has created a new magazine around the Old School look. *WM Brown* magazine debuted in 2019 and focuses on the romance of well-made men's clothes, and old Land Rovers. If the man in your life is fond of this sort of look, seek out an issue to present as a gift.

"The best vintage gift I ever gave my husband was a set of vintage blazer buttons from the famed Scottish golf course St. Andrews. They were on a used blazer that I found at a thrift shop," said Julia Berenson. "I cut them off and put them on one of his own blazers, and he gets nothing but jealous admiration from the guys who notice those kinds of details."

Interior designer and man-about-town Franklin John Kakies believes that vintage objects make the best gifts for both men and women. Old or new, there is nothing quite so flattering as a well-chosen gift, because it shows that the giver has been paying attention. But, when it comes to capital-R romance, nothing can beat a beautifully chosen vintage present! The fact that you cannot merely go out and buy something vintage or antique "off the peg" alone makes the gift seem more special, and when you couple that with the "well-chosen" part, the romance quotient increases manyfold!

Time Out

♥

You hear this advice daily, so you might as well hear it from us, too: tech devices in the bedroom at night are a very bad idea. Need to hear that again? Tech devices in the bedroom at night are a *very bad idea*! Not only because they prevent our brains from going into the slow-down-for-relaxation mode, and the blue light interferes with the production of much-needed melatonin, but also because they prevent us from reaching for each other at night. If you are holding your iPad in bed, you aren't holding your partner. Better to spend the evening wind-down time talking, or maybe follow our next romance recommendation and read to each other.

So try, try as hard as you can, to establish nighttime routines that leave your devices in another room.

"I think our iPads have interfered with our lovemaking," says one long-married woman who wishes to remain anonymous. "We used to reach for each other, but now . . . first thing in the morning and last thing at night we reach for our iPads. It makes me sad."

Story Time

♥

Rather than spend the last thirty minutes of your evening lying next to each other in bed looking at your iPads (and we know you do that because we do it, too), imagine how romantic it would be to take turns reading out loud to each other from a book you chose together. Elizabeth Austin and her husband, Russell, have made that their nighttime routine for years.

"The first book that my husband and I read aloud to each other was Ursula K. Le Guin's *The Left Hand of Darkness*. I don't remember many of the story's details now, but I do remember the quiet pleasures of being nineteen and snuggling with the man I loved on a bench in the waiting room of a train station somewhere in Scotland listening as his voice carried us together into worlds previously unknown.

After we married, many years passed before we resumed reading aloud to each other. As our two sons grew up, reading aloud to them was part of their go-to-bed routine. After they were both launched and living away from home, we began again. One of the first books that we chose was Ian McEwan's *Saturday*, a book that my husband had recently read and enjoyed so much he wanted to share it with me.

As we have grown older and sleep has become more elusive, reading aloud while tucked cozily in our bed has become a welcome bridge between wakefulness and slumber. We choose the books together from recent releases and old favorites. Among the books that we've read aloud over the last few years are Diana Gabaldon's *Outlander*, Charles Frazier's *Varina*, and Amor Towles's *A Gentleman in Moscow*. We read aloud every night almost without fail, even when traveling. Sharing a story is a great way to end the day on the same page!"

Sound like something you would enjoy making a part of your nighttime routine? Go ahead and give it a try!

Couch Surfing

Okay, maybe not exactly surfing, but couch traveling anyway. A recent travel magazine released a list of what their readers voted the best travel films of all time, and we agree. Why not take an evening trip to a faraway place from the comfort of your own home?

Here are a few of the top-rated travel films according to *Condé Nast Travel*:

To Catch a Thief (1955): Filmed in the south of France around Cannes and Nice, the scenery will make you want to book a trip tomorrow. Cary Grant and Grace Kelly and fabulous clothes and jewelry.

Two for the Road (1967): Audrey Hepburn and Albert Finney are also on a road trip to southern France, and the cars they drive will make you envious.

Murder on the Orient Express (1974): Hmmm, readers choose the older version over the remake that was released in 2017. Both versions include exotic travel scenes and the luggage to go with it.

Amélie (2001): A cheerful movie that puts Paris in a lovely light, with charming scenes in many neighborhoods.

Under the Tuscan Sun (2003): This film is based on a classic bestselling memoir, and you can sit in your living room and bask in the sights and sounds of the Italian countryside.

Away We Go (2009): A couple about to become parents visit several spots in the US in order to decide just where they want to raise their new baby.

Crazy Rich Asians (2018): Did you see it? You know you want to go and have a drink in the sky bar that keeps showing up. So if you haven't already dropped everything to visit Singapore (and tourism there is way up as a result of this film), why not visit it again from your own home? You'll be glad you did.

A Most Romantic Moment

In May of 1991, no air of sophistication surrounded me at all. I held far less eclectic taste in music than I do now, had never traveled outside the United States, and was busy finishing my last quarter at UC Davis in English as one of a handful of commuter students on campus. But in that youthful state, the truest and purest moment of romance I'd ever experienced happened, one that has yet to be replicated with the same sincerity or innocence. It begins—as I now believe all whimsical and lovely moments do—in a little café tucked away on a side street just off campus.

This particular spot featured Persian food like warm barley soup on cold and rainy Northern California winter days and refreshing cucumber and tomato salads when the unbearable heat of the Sacramento Valley hits in spring. I'd often hoist my poetry books over to this hole-in-the-wall and study over tea and treats, and this day was no different from any other. I ordered and opened a book.

As I read and waited for my repast to arrive, a tall, dark-haired, handsome man wearing a suit on this humid and sweltering day dropped a napkin by my novel and said, "You were so beautiful sitting there that I had to sketch you." He turned and walked out. I looked down to find an impressionistic-like sketch of me, barely looking down in my notebook, the flower on my spring hat etched in detail, my cupid-bow lips slightly smiling, a dimple present on my visage, cascading dark curls alive and brushing my shoulders. It may have been the best moment of my life as I realized that— even if for a few, fleeting minutes—I'd been someone's muse.

—Lynne Marie Rominger

Enshrined in History

♥

Picture this— There you are on a fabulous trip to Paris, gazing up at a star in the ceiling of the medieval French Abbey of Saint-Germain-des-Prés, knowing that it is the one you two paid for. Or perhaps you are out to the theater at a local playhouse and stepping over a brick in the entryway with your names on it. In almost every town, in almost every country, there are restoration projects that will allow you to give and see your name enshrined forever.

It is indeed a romantic gift to give in your names to help restore something that is centuries old in the hope that it will continue to stand for centuries in the future. Your love, your relationship, is now a stone on the building. A dab of mortar, an inch of steel beam, holding the world together.

Of course there are many worthy restoration projects closer to your own community, but if you do want to make the romantic gesture of helping out with the restoration of Notre Dame, check out the official French government website for links to sanctioned organizations. You can find them at gouvernement. fr under the heading "Let's Rebuild Together."

Clean the Garage (Again?!)

♥

Yes, sounds like an antiromantic downer of a way to spend a precious weekend day, but yes, it is in fact a positive way for a couple to rummage through their life together and reminisce. (Oh, look at this! Remember when we . . .) Decide jointly to discard, organize, and end the day feeling lighter and freer. What is antiromance though, is to start a big task and then leave it unfinished. A festering wound of a reminder, certain to breed resentment. So finish what you start.

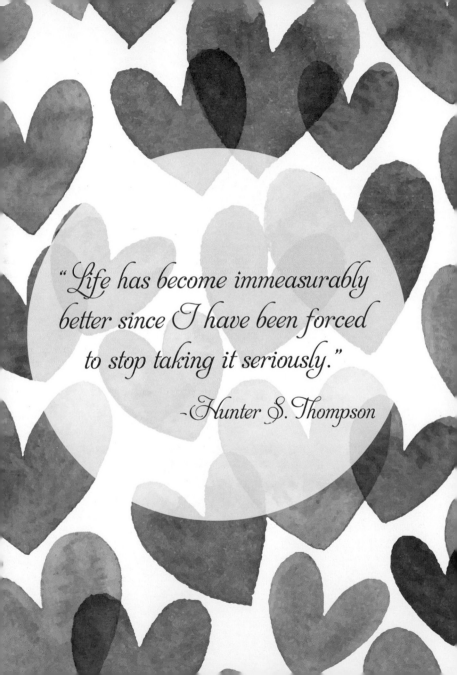

Step One . . .

♥

Assembling something like IKEA furniture together? Could be fun, could be fatal. A sense of joint accomplishment or a guarantee of a ruined evening? Could go either way, might as well accept it. You might have noticed a theme in many of the suggestions in this book—that romance and coupledom are strengthened when we work together as a team. So whenever the opportunity arises to try to put together a piece of furniture, or perhaps undergo a household repair or improvement, recognize from the beginning that things might get tense and agree to work through the moment. Who knows, it may ultimately become a treasured moment in your relationship, one to be reminisced over many times in the years to come.

On a romantic trip to an IKEA, you'd first have to go through the potential pitfalls of shopping there together (you might get lost and panic that you'll never find the exit . . . you might find out that your partner doesn't like Swedish meatballs!) and making a joint decision about what to buy. But the romantic adventure truly begins when you try to work together to assemble what you've bought . . .

IKEA as a romantic destination? In fact, some couples have even gotten married at an IKEA! More than 500 couples applied for the chance at a big group wedding in an IKEA in the US, and twenty lucky couples were chosen. And yes, meatballs were served at the reception.

A Most Romantic Moment

In the apple orchards in late fall, we went for an evening walk. He in his red-and-emerald tartan scarf and me in my almost-wintertime coat, our faces flushed pink in the cooling air. Sensing the romantic atmosphere of the occasion, we sought to do something spontaneous to mark it in our memory. Both of us, being of an environmentally conscious generation, decided not to carve our initials into the side of a tree trunk as past generations would have done. Instead, he cleared away a space beneath of one of the apple trees and, with gathered leaves of myriad autumn colors, spelled out our initials in the earth, encasing them in the shape of a heart made of gathered twigs.

Though far from the caliber of land art by the masterful Andy Goldsworthy, our little design did what we'd hoped: it made a lasting moment, special and lovely to remember. A reflection of affection, one season among many in our life together.

—Josiah Patterson

Get Real

♥

Men and women alike, we've all grown up with ideas on what love and romance and coupledom are supposed to look like. We get our messages from song lyrics, movie plots, commercials, novels, soap operas, and it all looks so great. All those dewy-eyed glances, all those warm embraces, all those happily-ever-afters—never an argument, never a sharp word, never a disappointment over a lackluster get-together . . . Yeah right. The more mature way to conduct a romance is to be clear-eyed about what real life is like.

So have realistic expectations. Don't set yourself up for disappointment by comparing your relationship to what appears (remember, looks can be deceiving) to be the idyllic romances that you think others are having. We all put on a good front before family and friends, so chances are their relationships are just as "real" as yours. Life isn't always smooth. Love isn't always smooth.

Fund Together, Right Now . . .

Have you ever dreamed of being an inventor? A movie producer? Product developer? In small ways, now you can be all of those things.

Gofundme.com and Kickstarter.com, among others, now give you the chance to help make amazing things possible. Why not scroll through the offerings and decide together as a couple whom you'd like to back? Sometimes you might get a commemorative t-shirt, but other times you might well see your name scroll by on the movie screen credits or be invited to an exclusive listening party for the release of some music you helped make possible. It might also open your eyes to the plethora of ways that businesses and creative projects get started nowadays. You two just might start creating a project of your own.

"Whatever you are,
be a good one."

-Abraham Lincoln

Be Fresh

♥

A gift of flowers has long been a signal for romance, but sometimes a bouquet from a florist can seem overly fussy and sterile. So why not make it a habit to casually pluck fresh flowers and present them to your love more regularly than ordering up a big bunch of expensive blooms? More often than not, the simple gesture packs more meaning than the grand one. Optimally, you will pluck flowers from your own yard to present, but there might also be opportunities to find an overgrown bush leaning into a forgotten alleyway or along a public street. And no need to gather up a full bouquet; just a single scented flower or even a lovely fallen leaf will do. No need to say anything when you present it, either. Just a smile as you offer a tiny gift of nature.

Flowers have meanings—centuries ago, lovers learned to send secret messages to each other through the various flowers they picked. Floriography (isn't that a pretty word?) reached its zenith in Victorian England. The deep red of some roses was meant to signify the intensity of romantic love, and purple violets meant the giver was preoccupied with thoughts of love. Tulips, on the other hand, represent passion. Two lips, perhaps?

A Most Romantic Moment

My wife is an engineer, and we joke that overtly sentimental or romantic gestures tend to be lost on her. But it really is just that—a joke. I make a point of sending flowers to her office a few times a year, and she says it is very romantic that even though I work from home and don't have a regular 9-to-5 schedule, I get up at 5:15 a.m. with her every morning and make her coffee just the way she likes it.

But when I asked her about a specific romantic moment, I was surprised at what she told me.

A few years ago, we both had work in Washington, DC. I flew out on a Friday morning, while she had a flight the following morning. They could not have been more different. I had just beat an incoming storm; she was right in the heart of it all. While it took me barely six hours even with a layover, canceled flights and closed airports left her stranded first in Salt Lake City and then in Boston before she finally arrived 36 hours after she had left, much of it sitting in a plane on the tarmac.

Worse, she was there to give a major presentation the next morning where her bosses and assorted other bigwigs would be in attendance. The delays had cost her all of her final prep time, and she was totally exhausted and stressed beyond words. And then she was looking at waiting around for another hour and a half at DCA for her boss, who insisted on picking her up.

I had a work event that afternoon, but I immediately begged off and surprised her at DCA. A few glasses of wine and the chance to tell me about the travails of her flights later, she was feeling much better.

I had no idea at the time it meant that much to her, but like the morning coffee, it is so often the little things that show the people in our lives that we love them.

—Rich Ehisen

Be Entertaining

♥

We are all on our best behavior when entertaining guests. We put on better clothes, use better manners, drink better wine, and make better and more interesting food than on an ordinary night. So for a somewhat more romantic life, maybe we should entertain more often . . . Find entertaining stressful? Do it anyway. The good news is that the more often you do it, the less stressful you will find it.

Antiestablishment

♥

Established routines are comfortable, and every couple develops them over time. Maybe you go for a walk together every Sunday in the same park, or visit the farmers market on Saturday mornings. Cozy. Sweet. And a tradition that should be kept intact. But what if . . . one Saturday you went to the farmers market in the next town instead? Or to a u-pick farm in the next county? Because routines are lovely, but having new experiences together is what builds memories and adds a measure of excitement to our daily lives. Whichever routine you have fallen in together as a couple, whether it is a romantic ritual or a mundane task, every so often you should try to mix it up and keep things fresh.

Brain plasticity, now there's a sexy term—not. But it is an idea you should always reach for. It refers to the brain's natural ability to grow and change, and brain plasticity continues into adulthood as we learn new information and experience new things. So get out there and start stretching your brain.

Be a Maker

♥

We all love to receive gifts, regardless of the occasion. There is also a great deal of joy in giving gifts. Giftgiving can break the bank pretty quickly, though. Is there a way we can go beyond the idea of spending money on gifts? "Make them things" was the romantic advice given by a 20-year-old college junior when quizzed about the best way to show love and affection. In many ways, making a gift for someone is even more lavish than spending vast sums of money on jewelry or electronics or whatever the newest thing might be. Make a meal, make some art, write a simple poem.

What makes a handmade gift an authentic expression of affection is not only that it is a one-of-a-kind object (made by you!), but also that you got to spend time thinking about the recipient while you were working on it. Knitting a long scarf? Hours and hours of time to think about the person you are making it for. Baking a batch of brownies for a chocolate lover? The warmly delicious smell wafting through the house while they bake helps you anticipate their delighted reaction when you present the plate.

"*Love is or it ain't.
Thin love ain't love at all.*"

-Toni Morrison

Practice Your Moods

♥

"Act as if" is a piece of advice from more than one motivational speaker. It usually is used when giving career advice, like "Act as if you were already the CEO!" or "Act as if you had already founded a successful start-up!" But what if we were to "act as if" when we are in a truly romantic situation/moment/relationship place? Our minds and our moods are connected.

Close your eyes and picture the most romantic setting you can imagine. Maybe it is a scene you once saw in a travel magazine, an isolated two-person rustic hut built on stilts over the achingly blue ocean. Or a well-worn and slightly run-down Italian villa on the edge of a canal in Venice. Feel the moist air on your skin. In the same meditative way we are encouraged to picture a babbling brook or a field of waving lavender in order to fall asleep, use the same technique to manifest a romantic mood.

In Chambers

♥

Classical music is almost always the soundtrack for love and romance. At weddings, we walk down the aisle to Mendelssohn's Wedding March or Pachelbel's Canon in D, in movies there is always a little Ravel's Bolero playing in the background . . . but actually attending a classical symphony performance isn't always everyone's thing. Instead, why not seek out some chamber music? It might be easier to get your partner on board with the idea of attending a concert in a less overwhelming fancy dress setting.

Symphonies are played by big symphony orchestras, sometimes close to a hundred musicians for a big Beethoven. Chamber music, on the other hand, was designed to be played in a smaller setting, by fewer musicians. Literally in a chamber, a room. Sometimes the room was in a palace, but just as likely in a drawing room of a smaller home.

Where would you find chamber music in your area? Because chamber musicians perform in smaller spaces, look at local museums and art galleries, city halls, and other civic spaces.

A Most Romantic Moment

It all began innocently enough. Freshly sprung from wildly inappropriate marriages, we both had unwittingly shown up at the moral equivalent of a Herbalife party. Later, he handed me his number on a torn piece of paper plate. 'Let's have coffee, I'm an architect,' he said, hoping to communicate that he was in no way a member of the vitamin-selling ranks. Six months later, we had fallen hopelessly in love.

As divorced forty-somethings, it took just moments of contemplating the mash-up of our two huge families, and the months of planning, spending, and unparalleled stress of another wedding, for us to cry, "Let's elope!"

How about Spain?

But the wedding dress—How to do it? Transport, more luggage, shlepping it around Europe afterward?—no. Jogging in our neighborhood park later, a thrift store dress and suitcase seemed the only solution.

Leaving the park to run home, we caught sight of a garage sale. Something was hanging from a tree, and as we approached, we realized that it was, oddly enough, a wedding dress. And some cardboard boxes . . . No one around, we knocked on the door. "Is this a garage sale?"

"No . . .," replied the woman who answered.

"But the wedding dress, is that for sale?"

"No," she replied. "That's for you. Bring it back if it doesn't fit. But it's going to fit." She smiled and closed the door.

With trembling fingers, my lover buttoned up the forty satin buttons in the back, pulling the '60s-style scalloped lace tight across my bare shoulders. I held my breath. Did I mention that I was already with child?

Don't get the wrong idea—we were legally married. We had run to City Hall on New Year's Eve, and now we had a little one coming, eight weeks along. This dress needed to fit! For two more weeks!

The last button closed perfectly. We left California that weekend, clutching a little Calistoga bottle with garden roses for our "bouquet." Outside of Barcelona, we found a lovely old estate, abandoned for years, donated to the city, full of paths, fountains, and the requisite pillars we brides seem to crave.

After saying our vows, we walked over to the fountain one last time. Softly, quietly, almost imperceptibly, the rain began to fall. As we scattered the petals from the roses from our little garden in

California, a lovely thing happened—one raindrop fell into each petal, like a tiny cup just capable of holding one sacred drop.

We ran for the rental car, laughing at the unstateliness of it all—wedding dress dragging, flowers sagging, tux flapping—and got in just as it began to fall in earnest.

Back at the hotel, we picked up our bags and prepared the dress for the last stop in its long journey from California. We pinned a note to the front that read, "This dress comes to you from California, worn with love—Free to a woman of good spirit." Thank God I married a Cuban who knew how to phrase this in Spanish.

And there in Barcelona, we left it hanging on a tree, in a lovely park. We thanked our lucky stars every day that we had found each other in this big wide world. And hoped that like us, some lucky lovers would find "The Dress."

—Julie Didion

The Doctor Will
See You (Both) Now

♥

No one should have to go to a doctor's appointment alone; it can be a very stressful experience. Is a doctor's office really a romantic setting? Okay, hard to picture that as a romantic environment, but it is a place to over and over again show your dedication to another person. Think about your own mood when you go to a doctor's appointment—either you are worried in advance over the outcome and would love someone there to reassure you, or you end up with happy news and wish you had someone nearby to share it with. And let's be honest, in stressful situations, it always helps to have a second pair of ears to make sure you have fully comprehended the information.

So no, a joint visit to the doctor's office is far from romantic but it shows day in and day out commitment to your relationship. You both plan to be there for the mundane moments as well as the exciting ones.

Healthy Together

♥

A great way to show your love is meant to last a lifetime is to make sure that your body will last a lifetime, too. Healthy eating is a visible way to show your love to each other.

No one likes a nag, and no one enjoys being lectured. We all know this, so try not to make the idea of healthy eating a point of contention. And healthy eating looks different for every one of us. For some, it is eating and drinking what they want in moderation; for others, it might be a strict vegan approach. Understand that you and your partner might have different approaches to healthy eating and make peace with that.

And although the old expression "A way to a man's heart is through his stomach" typically meant spaghetti and cake and pie, now it really means kale and smoothies. Feeling overly full isn't romantic. No one wants to snuggle up on the couch if their waistband is digging in after a big heavy meal.

Get a Clue

♥

Looking for a simple and fun way to give a gift to your partner? Grab a pencil and blank paper or fire up a design program on your computer and create a custom crossword puzzle. Doesn't that sound like a great way to acknowledge an anniversary or birthday?

Write your message out first in an empty grid pattern and then figure out the personalized clues that draw from your experiences together. Can you picture that? It is as though you were writing a message on a Scrabble board. The words need to work and make sense in both directions. There is no need to make it super fancy; making it by hand just adds to the heartwarming charm. Word of warning on the clues, though try not to make them too obscure. You don't need this gift to end up hurting feelings if someone doesn't remember your mother's middle name or what kind of wine you drank on your first date. Make it fun and relatively easy, not a total memory test.

A Most Romantic Moment

My golden girl was dying. Instead of our daily run in the foothills, we had substituted long, slow walks on the grassy fields that lined a major boulevard. I couldn't bear to keep her indoors.

A chiseled, ponytailed man approached us that May morning in 1994. It was as though he had appeared out of nowhere. I hadn't seen him amble toward us from the far side of the field, where people were flying kites.

"What a beautiful golden retriever," he said. I replied, "Thank you. Unfortunately, she has kidney failure." He squatted down to pet her. She leaned against him as if she had known him from another life. "What's her name?" he asked. I answered, "B.J., short for Bonnie Jean."

We sat on the grass talking for eight hours while B.J. slept between us. B.J. died five days before we married the following autumn.

One year had passed since B.J.'s death. I was feeling sorry for myself after a long day of teaching. I couldn't believe Glenn hadn't mentioned the importance of this day before we left for work that morning. After all, B.J. had brought us together. Glenn was unusually late, and I was concerned. When he finally walked through the front door, I was annoyed. He didn't even say hello as he ducked down the hallway with a package in his hands. "Jeaninne," he

called. "Come into the den." I purposefully took my time. When I turned into the room, Glenn was standing in front of the blonde IKEA cabinet. He nodded toward the top shelf. A simple pine box with a bronze plaque sat in the center of the shelf. I looked up and read the inscription: B.J., MOMMY LOVES YOU. AUGUST 1983– NOVEMBER 1994. Glenn had never forgotten.

—Jeaninne Escallier Kato

"I love you for all that you are,
all that you have been, all that
you're yet to be."

-Ernest Hemingway

Side by Side

♥

Side-by-side pedicures: go for it! Your partner might object initially, but trust me, if you can get them to do this once, you will never have to cajole again. Slip your feet into the warm foot bath, relax while warm oil is massaged, no one will want to give that up. Shared experiences are the best, and sharing an hour-long indulgence might become a monthly habit. Yes, couples' massages are also a nice indulgence, but that is more of an "in the same room but not interacting" kind of thing. With side-by-side pedicures, you can talk, hold hands, or just sit and smile at each other while enjoying the attention being paid to your feet.

Not everyone will want to go all in for the nail polish, although even the most macho may be cajoled into giving it a try. All it will take to undo it is a quick swipe of nail polish remover . . .

A Most Romantic Moment

Newly single, I'd received a number of conciliatory "It happens when you least expect it" platitudes from friends, but it turns out they were right. As my Southwest flight to California was about to leave Denver, a handsome someone filled the middle seat and courteously stowed his bag under the seat in front of him, leaving nowhere to stretch his long legs. I couldn't help but strike up a conversation.

As fate would have it, he was single, and the more we talked, the more we discovered we had in common. We'd worked for and been laid off by the same company, were left-handed, and preferred to sleep in total darkness to the extent that we covered up LEDs in the room. We were both hopelessly blunt, introverted, and the oldest child, and we'd both lived in the same Bay Area town. We talked for three hours straight, ignoring the books in our laps and barely seeing each other's faces because we were facing forward.

Sensing that this could be a once-in-a-lifetime connection, I knew I had to get his phone number, so I hatched a little plan. The plane was being deiced (something that may happen a lot in Colorado, but not in California; I was intrigued). I took a picture out the window of the deicing in progress, then asked if he wanted me to text him the photo. To my delight, he fell for it.

It's been five months, and I've since learned that he was thrilled I asked for his phone number because he was too shy to ask for mine. He's definitely the love of my life. In tribute to how we met, when we go out to restaurants, we often sit side by side in "airplane mode."

—Catherine Dee

Simply Delicious

♥

For a deliciously romantic dessert, the limoncello and vanilla ice cream recipe from Ina Garten, the Barefoot Contessa, is hard to beat. Rather than stress out trying to make something fancy and complicated, go ahead and invest in a bottle of limoncello. It will last and last, and you will smile each time you spot it in your cupboard as the launch pad for many a night snuggled up on the couch watching a favorite show and enjoying the indulgent flavors and textures of a scoop of rich vanilla ice cream and a drizzle of decadent limoncello on top. And as is always the case, the light dessert, rather than a heavy one, will leave you more in the mood for late night love and romance. The "recipe" is in Ina Garten's book, *Cook Like a Pro*, but it is just a description of pouring a shot of the lemon-flavored liquor on top of a scoop of high-quality vanilla ice cream. Don't fancy lemon flavor? Then why not just pour a drizzle of your favorite after-dinner drink? Bailey's Irish Cream would do the trick nicely, too!

Literary Adventurers

♥

Do you have a favorite book? What is your partner's favorite book? A novel, perhaps, or a work of history? You can bring that book to life and create an entire adventure around it. Plan a trip to the setting of your partner's favorite book. What a great way to get creative about how to recreate it!

Or create an afternoon based around a famous book like *The Maltese Falcon*. In San Francisco, the café John's Grill on Ellis Street is decorated in homage to the fact that the writer Dashiell Hammett spent time there and used it as a setting in the book.

If you find yourself in Paris (lucky you!) and you are traveling with a Harry Potter fan, why not seek out the oldest house in Paris, the home of the real-life Nicolas Flamel?

While in Chicago, be sure and head out to the suburb of Oak Park and wander the same streets that Ernest Hemingway did as a young boy, not to mention the other famed Oak Park resident, architect Frank Lloyd Wright.

New Orleans is full of literary hobby holes like the bar at the Hotel Monteleone, where Truman Capote and Tennessee Williams were known to drink.

Ready to tour the bookshops and libraries of Paris and London? Check out the literary tour company Mitford Maugham and see if there is a trip for you and your partner: mitfordmaugham.com

A Most Romantic Moment

When our son was nearing three years old, I sat my husband down to tell him I needed more help from him with household chores and taking care of our child. I'd given a lot of thought to how to frame the discussion in a way that was constructive and not mean-spirited. But the conversation exploded and became a tirade by both of us on how we didn't pay attention to each other's needs anymore. My husband felt ignored and left out of my life, including my relationship with our son. I didn't understand why he didn't try harder to find ways to help around the house and with our child's care. We sat back, a bit stunned, and a little uncertain if we could find our way back to being more than a mom and a dad.

We booked a babysitter and a reservation at an Italian restaurant in hopes that date nights would help us wind our way back to each other. I put on a dress. Conversation was stilted—we were not certain that we'd finished the grenade throwing. As we waited for dessert, I went to the ladies' room. When I returned, I picked up my napkin from the table and found a small black velvet box. I cried looking at the diamond stud earrings, and my husband's warm green eyes were wet. He wasn't done with us, and neither was I.

—Marianne Lonsdale

Game Night

♥

Need a new way to spend time together other than side by side on the couch watching Netflix? Pull out the board games and have at it. Create a new family tradition of playing board games, either just as a couple or by inviting another couple over to amp up the competition. Because if you win as a team, you can celebrate together later in the evening. And if you lose, you can console each other over the loss. Either way, it will be an experience you had together, and that is (almost always) a good thing. Add some old-fashioned comfort food to the mix, and you have a nice nostalgic tradition. Forget the avocado toast and sushi and go for sour cream onion dip and ruffled chips! Tiny meatballs on toothpicks! All of the things your grandmother might have prepared as finger foods.

If board games don't excite you as a couple, seek out a trivia night at a bar or pub near you. Trivia nights generally draw their questions from a wide variety of topics—geography, sports, history, pop culture, and so on—so there might be a category in which each of you can shine. Because, admit it, it is always a thrill to show off in front of your partner.

"Tabletop games," as the category is known, are surging in popularity. Check out the top-funded section of Kickstarter.com: over 900 million dollars has been pledged in that category by ordinary folks like you. So maybe that is also an idea for romantic togetherness: don't just play the game, fund the game!

Romantic Splurges

"Where do you want to go?"

"Oh, I don't know, where do you want to go?"

"What do you want to do?"

"I don't know, what do you want to do?"

You've had this same conversation many times, haven't you? It might be about a restaurant, a movie, or your next vacation. Sometimes couples find it hard to come up with new ideas. Despite all the choices that surround us, we tend to fall back on the same ones time and again. *How about that cabin on the coast we go to every summer, the café where they serve that great salad, the movie that the neighbors recommended . . .?*

Here's an idea: Why not shake things up and do something entirely out of character for you two? Something to startle your friends, amaze your children, and bring you closer together as a couple?

Travel dreams, family hopes, or secret personal goals: every life is filled with possibility! Here are five great (but pretty spendy) bucket-list items for couples to dream about together, either late at night over a glass of champagne or on a lazy Sunday morning while lounging in bed:

1. Have dinner up in the Eiffel Tower: Picture this—the two of you leaning in close over the table, gazing out the window at Paris in all its glory. Jules Verne, a restaurant with both a new chef at the helm and a newly remodeled interior, is literally tops for romance. Not only is the food wonderful, but you can skip the lines and whisk up the tower in a private elevator that is reserved for diners.

2. Attend a masked ball in Venice: You've seen this in movies, read about it in novels. All those elegantly dressed Europeans in elaborate masks twirling on the dance floor is so romantic. And so within reach! You can buy the tickets and rent the costumes at the same time at venice-carnival-italy.com. Plan on it for next year at this same time. The good news is that over-crowded Venice isn't nearly as overcrowded in the winter.

3. Learn to cook another language: Speak another language, cook another language, experience life in another language. Attending a cooking class together in a foreign country will immerse you in the food, the language, and the culture in an incredible way. A week-long cooking class in a 16th-century castle in Italy would certainly do the trick: awaitingtable.com.

4. Get silly at clown school: Laughter is infectious. Trusting each other enough to do something goofy is an important step in any relationship. Camp Winnarainbow has been going on for more than forty years, founded by famed '60s hippie figure Wavy

Gravy. Located up on the California coast, it offers sessions as short as a few days or as long as a week. Juggling, trapeze skills, clowning—this is the place for adults to let loose and experience their inner clown: campwinnarainbow.org.

5. Live in a castle: Live for free in a grand place in Europe for a week or a month or more in exchange for taking care of the pets while the owner travels? Sure, you can handle that together. A recent listing on the website Trustedhousesitters.com is for a seven-bedroom historic stone farm in Southern France with "breathtaking" views of the Pyrenees.

Open up and share your dream destination with your loved one; maybe they share the same dream, and soon you could be headed there, together!

Contributors

Jennifer Aldrich is an author, performer, and event planner. She is a board member of the Adventuresses' Club of the Americas, a nonprofit that produces Miss Fisher Con, the annual convention for fans of Miss Fisher's Murder Mysteries. The third successful occurrence of this annual event was recently held in San Jose, California.

Julia Berenson is the pen name of an author who has written an unseemly number of books and therefore wishes to spare the reading public the trauma of seeing her name yet again.

Laura Boswell began her career as a sportswriter and has written articles and essays for many national publications and outlets like *USA Today*, NPR, and ESPN. She is currently working on a novel about the greed behind African trophy hunting. She lives in Bowling Green, Kentucky, with her boyfriend, Wes, his three lovely daughters, and the world's dumbest (but cutest) Basset Hound, Moe.

Catherine Dee is an editor and the author of a series of empowering books for girls and young women, including *The Girls' Book of Wisdom.* She lives in Orangevale, California.

Julie Didion is a painter, sculptor, and former buyer and illustrator for a chain of high-fashion shoe boutiques. Her work has been exhibited in galleries in Sacramento, San

Francisco, the Sonoma Valley, Los Angeles, and Washington, DC and appears in private collections in Sacramento, San Francisco, Los Angeles, New York, Paris, and Helsinki.

Karen Durham is a happy California writer. She's had short stories, poems, and creative nonfiction published, including spoken word. Along with writing, she has, with her 28-year love, run across Cloud's Rest in Yosemite and twice swum from Alcatraz to San Francisco. Her blog is called Kiki Knows.

Rich Ehisen is an award-winning journalist, editor, and public speaker who has spent more than twenty-five years interviewing and reporting on politicians, athletes, authors, CEOs, celebrities, artists, cops, doers, and dreamers all over the country. He is the managing editor of the *State Net Capitol Journal*, a LexisNexis publication that covers all 50 statehouses, and his freelance work has appeared in a variety of publications across the country.

Pam Giarrizzo is the creator of The Booktrekker blog, exploring the world through books, food, and giving. She and her husband, Phil, split their time between Northern California and Medellin, Colombia.

Franklin John Kakies lives in solitary bachelor splendor with too many chairs (all of them antique) and collections ranging from Billiken (*The God of Things As They Ought to Be*) to Georgian silver. Among his all-time favorite presents he numbers a late 18th-century Irish Georgian mahogany dumbwaiter, a Modernistic c. 1930 wheel, an acid-cut glass lamp depicting life under the sea, and a set of (vintage) sterling silver luggage labels.

Jeaninne Escallier Kato is a retired bilingual educator who finds her writing muse in the Mexican culture. She is the author of the children's book *Manuel's Murals*, a love letter to her Mexican American students. Jeaninne is published in several anthologies for her short memoirs and flash fiction work. She is also a contest winner for her fictional story "A Desert Rose." Jeaninne lives in Northern California with her husband, Glenn, and three rescued fur babies.

Remy Kenney launched Honeyfitz Yacht Club in October of 2018, which is an e-commerce retail shop celebrating the best of coastal style. From vintage nautical flags to retro lawn chairs, Honeyfitz has curated the store especially for those who thrive on understatement and a strong cocktail at the end of the day. Remy lives in Charleston, South Carolina, with her husband, Matt, and her daughters, Reese and Charlotte: honeyfitzyachtclub.com.

JT Long has written for books, magazines, websites, and once on a gas station bathroom wall, but only because there was a grammar mistake on the sign, and she happened to have a red pen handy.

Marianne Lonsdale writes personal essays, fiction, and literary interviews. Her work has been published in *Literary Mama*, *Grown and Flown*, and *Pulse* and has aired on KQED. Marianne has read at various events including San Francisco's Litquake festival and is honored to be an alumna of the Community of Writers at Squaw Valley. Additional information can be found at mariannelonsdale.com.

Ingrid Lundquist is a creative spirit. After a career as a Certified Special Events Professional, she took up photography in 2011 and since then has been in more than 70 juried shows across the US and abroad. She is the author of three business books on event production, a photo story book, and two books related to self-publishing. Learn more about Ingrid at IngridLundquist.com.

Ruben Mauricio is a recently retired Special Education teacher of 33 years. He is now focusing on his next adventure, writing the libretto for his bilingual opera "Respiro / I Breathe," which takes place in 1960s Southwest Detroit, and focuses on Santiago, a son of Mexican and Polish immigrants who imagines a different life for himself.

Angela Montanez is a health & fitness rebel, Channeler Mediyum, psychic, old soul, energy worker, and plant-based foodie in New York City. She is the lead MediYum, wellness rebel girl, and fit-fashion blogger at basicbitchstyle.com. You can find her at angelamontanez.com. Angela resides in New York City with her family and two dogs.

Josiah Patterson was born and raised in Montana and has been a published writer, guardian ad litem, special education teacher, and late night bus bouncer. He has put down roots in many places around the world, including Prague and, most recently, with his family in Sacramento, California. He is a casual poet and occasional proser. His writing endeavors span a wide list of interests, from an appreciation of nature to a healthy curiosity in the supernatural.

Andrea Riso, GG, AGS, is the proprietor/designer at Talisman Collection Fine Jewelers in El Dorado Hills, CA: talismancollection.com.

Lynne Marie Rominger is a Northern California educator, an author/coauthor of numerous books, and a contributor in several essay collections. She has also written more than 400 magazine and newspaper articles for local and national publications. When not teaching or writing, she enjoys nature, travel, her Eastern Orthodox faith, and spending time with her first grandchild.

Rita Taggert is an actress and cinematographer. Among her many screen credits are *Coming Home* (1978), *The China Syndrome* (1979), and *Mulholland Drive* (2001), as well as appearances in many popular television series like *Northern Exposure* and *Coach*. Her husband of many years, Oscar-winning cinematographer Haskell Wexler, passed away in 2015.